THE SUPERNATURAL

I0473918

By Lord Loveday Ememe and available from Lulu.
The constitution and policing
Heresy
Starfleet

Table of Contents

1. SUCCESS LINKED TO THE SUPERNATURAL

The purpose of the law or laws is to regulate the activities of the supernatural or the uncivilized (those with supernatural powers and senses).The law encourages little or no use of supernatural powers and senses. This means according to the guidance of the constitution, everything should be in good working order to limit the need or use of supernatural powers and senses .The purpose of the law is to mold the supernatural or uncivilized (those with supernatural powers and senses) into the likeness of the natural or civilized (those without supernatural powers and senses), in order to establish and maintain peace and security. The activities or behaviors of the supernatural have to mirror those of the natural, to maintain peace and security. The supernatural are in the habit of initiating unwanted or uninvited relationships with the civilized or natural , in order to oppress or dominate the civilized contrary to the guidance of the constitution .These unwanted relationships are created with the misuse of the supernatural powers and senses of the uncivilized. In order to justify the creation of these relationships, the uncivilized misuse their supernatural powers and senses to create problems in the lives of the civilized to give the false impression that their interest in the civilized is for a good purpose. In order to maintain these forced relationships, the supernatural misuse their supernatural powers and senses to make the lives of the civilized hell, contrary to the guidance of the constitution.

The constitution in its guidance , confirms that the use of supernatural powers and senses will have damaging psychological effects on the civilized , even when the supernatural believe that its use is for a good purpose .This is the reason the constitution insists on the immediate implementation of the necessary conditions for the civilized to enjoy our civil rights .This eliminates the need for the constant use of supernatural powers and senses by the uncivilized.

These forced unwanted relationships, imposed on the civilized by the uncivilized, come with rules for the civilized to obey, contrary to the constitution. These rules that are unconstitutional are meant to give the false impression of the superiority of the supernatural or the uncivilized, contrary to the guidance of the constitution. This superiority complex of the uncivilized accounts for the lack of restraint or lack of respect for the right to privacy of the civilized.

The constitution requires the uncivilized to align their behaviors to those of the civilized. The civilized, naturally respects everyone's right to privacy. The civilized are naturally incapable of violating the right to privacy .The violation of the right to privacy of the civilized by the misuse of supernatural powers and senses of the uncivilized , is not only illegal , immoral , it is also very unhealthy for the civilized , psychologically .Because the civilized are naturally nice (civil) and cannot say no in the language of the uncivilized , the uncivilized mistake that for consent.

According to the guidance of the constitution, the decision to create life is a decision that cannot be made lightly .The planet was meant for one individual, Adam; this suggests the standard that has been set to meet the needs of an individual. But the supernatural make decisions to create life lightly, without any consideration of how the needs of the individual can be met and how this decision will affect the lives of the civilized, given the guidance of the constitution.

According to the guidance of the constitution, everything came into existence supernaturally but took on the civilized natural form. According to the guidance of the constitution, the supernatural represent lawlessness (disorder).

The civilized naturally are not intrusive. The civilized are naturally independent. We the civilized will not naturally know anything about anyone, unless they or the supernatural want us to know. According to the guidance of the constitution, the civilized have dominion over this planet. This means that its natural resources belong to the civilized. The civilized will naturally not interfere with access to these resources. This is because we are not intrusive.

The constitution requires that the living conditions of the civilized should be aligned to the conditions in the Garden of Eden. This is why the civilized are naturally commissioners of police. The civil nature of the civilized entitles us to civil rights that were formulated in the Garden of Eden, and as a consequence the conditions in the modern world should be aligned so that we can benefit from our civil rights. When the supernatural or the uncivilized , use their supernatural powers and senses to compromise the independence of the civilized or the natural , by altering our living conditions in order to make decisions for the civilized directly or indirectly , their self-destructive assumptions of what they think the civilized will want will be based on their supernatural instincts. These assumptions will turn out to be very hostile for the civilized, and will be categorized as the misuse of supernatural powers and senses by the uncivilized to violate the civil rights of the civilized, because of its harmful effects.

The supernatural or the uncivilized behave like heroin addicts that need the discomfort of the vulnerable to cater to their uncivilized (barbaric) nature. The way that they achieve this is to try to force their way into people's lives by misusing their supernatural powers and senses to create problems or to make an issue of something they are aware of because of their supernatural senses and make a problem of the issue, politicize them, in order to give the uncivilized things to do at the expense of the physical and mental wellbeing of the vulnerable. According to the guidance of the constitution, the supernatural or the uncivilized are required to tailor their behavior to be similar to the behavior of the natural or civilized as a measure or gauge of success, in order to establish and maintain peace and security. But the supernatural or the uncivilized have conspired collectively to misinterpret the guidance of the constitution, and have linked success to the supernatural contrary to the guidance of the constitution. This practice by the uncivilized, according to the guidance of the constitution is disruptive and encourages lawlessness and the persecution of the vulnerable.

My personal experiences with the supernatural or the uncivilized have taught me that developing personal relationships with the supernatural is not advisable. The guidance of the constitution , with regard to the strict protocols for the uncivilized to follow to initiate or to have contact with the civilized, coupled with the self-destructive stubbornness of the supernatural , can be interpreted as meaning that contact with the civilized is not allowed. Given the supernatural nature of the uncivilized, contact includes the indirect and direct types of contact, supernaturally and naturally (because it is unregulated, as a consequence of the wrong identification, interpretation and application of the law and puts the civilized in danger of physical or mental abuse).

The audacity of the supernatural to create a culture contrary to the guidance of the constitution that links success to the supernatural is as a result of their false sense of self-importance resulting from their false sense of superiority.

The word metropolitan, with regard to the metropolitan police force, means civilization, the police force is meant to establish and maintain law and order according to the guidance of constitution of the United Kingdom, which is the Christian principles, civil rights .This police force is required by the constitution to align the living conditions of the modern world to that in the garden of Eden in the Christian teachings. This police force can only be commissioned by the civilized or the natural as commissioners of police, and assisted by the supernatural. The supernatural according to the guidance of the constitution, cannot be commissioners of police, even if they pretend to be civilized (those without supernatural powers and senses). The requirement of the sacred constitution is that the civilized or the natural must be commissioners of police. The supernatural as commissioners of police according to the guidance of the constitution will only attract living conditions outside the Garden of Eden, which is hell.

This sacred requirement cannot be undermined by the games and jokes associated with the self-destructive supernatural instincts of the uncivilized.

The supernatural rely on their supernatural instincts by ignoring the guidance of the constitution and as a consequence find the prospect of life (the real natural life span) daunting. The reasons for the problem is their associates or those they believe are their acquaintances, the type of life they have been drawn into or are living .Which is definitely a self-destructive wicked existence. These are psychological problems that can be resolved by counseling and getting away from the situation and getting away from the bad influences of their associates or acquaintances.

The constitution's guidance on peace and security with the instruction for the supernatural to tailor their behavior to the likeness of the civilized or the natural, is meant to help them enjoy the pleasures of life and to prevent criminal behavior or activity associated with the possible misuse of their supernatural powers and senses. The likeness of the civilized means , the characteristics of the civilized nature with regard to respect for independence , right to privacy, respect for financial security and independence, respect for law and order ,the natural respect for life, freedom of movement , the civilized are not naturally intrusive, respect for the good health of others, respect for agelessness etc.

The supernatural or the uncivilized, whose supernatural instincts are to inflict mental or physical injuries unprovoked on others, in particular the vulnerable, are not allowed under any circumstances to makes decisions for other people or to govern. They are required by the guidance of the constitution only to follow the orders of the natural or the civilized. The supernatural are so destructive that they have to create conditions to enable the continuous infliction of mental and physical injuries on others unprovoked. Wickedness is the natural instinct of the supernatural or the uncivilized even when they believe they are helping you or make you believe they are trying to help you. Their approach to problem solving will be guided by their supernatural instinct, which will end up being more harmful to the person being helped or the situation that they are trying to correct. The supernatural allow themselves to be drawn into the culture of lawlessness by conspiracy of action or inaction. This is easy to achieve because of their supernatural instincts, the prospects initially are exciting, to attack each other unprovoked with no repercussions if the attacker or victim is killed. This becomes a way of life. The problem for the supernatural is when the excitement wears off, and they are faced with unprovoked attacks on a regular basis. This then becomes hell for them, because they cannot walk away from the culture because of their past deeds .The young of the supernatural are initiated into this culture or way of life. This way of life accounts for the complete lack of self- respect amongst the supernatural, which makes them dangerous to themselves and those around them. Because of their wrong interpretation of the law and the lawless culture they have immersed themselves in, they appear to be unaware of the revulsion of a real civilized society towards those amongst the supernatural that misuse their supernatural powers and senses, directly or indirectly to harm mentally or physically the civilized or to breach the peace in a civilized society. The revulsion is worse than that society has towards rapists and pedophiles. They behave like pedophiles that only have each other as companions or acquaintances, with false confidence associated with the delusion brought about by the lack of awareness of the societal reaction of revulsion towards their type.

The supernatural or the uncivilized are in the habit of expecting the civilized to figure things out supernaturally, which is impossible, rather than the civilized option of explaining things properly. This strange behavior accounts for their expectations that the civilized will want to get involved in unhealthy, illegal role plays. The constitution requires the supernatural or the uncivilized to aspire to the qualities or characteristics of the civilized and not the other way round.

The practices of the supernatural misinterpreting the constitution in the guise of churches, mosques and synagogues, advocate that the civilized should aspire to the disorderly, disruptive characteristics of the supernatural.

The disorderly, disruptive nature of the supernatural or the uncivilized is evident with their efforts at entertainment; they have to use the characteristics or qualities of the civil nature for films, music, radio and television. They will find it difficult to complete a scene in a film if they decide to use their supernatural characteristics.

It is a very serious criminal matter when the supernatural try to trivialize civil rights, by supernaturally getting involved in the concerns of the civilized in the guise of games and jokes, because of the limited intellect of the supernatural with regard to civil rights.

As someone of a civilized nature, given my experiences with regard to the collective deception of the supernatural to undermine my civil rights before and after becoming aware of the existence of the differences in their supernatural or uncivilized natures and my civilized nature, I have doubts about the circumstances that led to Adam losing his civil rights. Adam, according to the guidance of the constitution immediately had dominion over this planet; the original plan was that the planet was meant for only him. Adam immediately had the constitutional authority as God. Then there was the Introduction of Eve, without consulting or the consent of Adam. The subsequent events could be interpreted as a conspiracy by the supernatural collectively, including Eve, to compromise the civil nature of Adam in order to undermine his civil rights, including his constitutional authority as God.

The supernatural are by nature extremely wicked, the differences in their nature and the nature of the civilized, means that attacks on the civilized by the supernatural are unprovoked.

The disaster in the garden of Eden in the Christian teachings according to the guidance of the constitution confirms that when the supernatural compromises the civil nature of the civilized, in order to undermine the civil rights of the civilized ,it is a conspiracy of the supernatural collectively to create hell on earth ,contrary to the instructions of the constitution.

The conspiracy of the supernatural or the uncivilized to create hell on earth by ignoring the instructions of the constitution by allowing their supernatural instincts to guide them is evident with the unconstitutional culture linking success to the supernatural in all aspects of life. This conspiracy helps their unconstitutional agenda to compromise or alter the civil nature of the civilized.

The celebrity associated with success in sports, implies that to be a winner in sports you need to be transformed from the natural to the supernatural. The celebrity associated with success in quiz shows or being a quiz show host encourages linking success to transforming the natural to the supernatural. The concept of celebrity, approval of the civilized through the supernatural or by the supernatural encourages the misconception that the supernatural are superior to the civilized. Celebrity associated with the enhanced sense of sight of the supernatural, and the importance given to the supernatural sense of sight in the guise of celebrity or the media encourages an indirect type of slavery to the opinions of the supernatural which is a deliberate misinterpretation of the constitution. The unconstitutional culture linking success to the supernatural nature is a deliberate persecution of the civilized. This culture ensures that the civilized will never be successful. The civilized will have to settle for being at the mercy of the supernatural for scraps for survival. Given the supernatural instincts of the supernatural or the uncivilized, their natural wicked nature or instincts will mean that life will be hell for the civilized, contrary to the instructions of the constitution.

2. HELL IS LAWLESSNESS

According to the guidance of the constitution the supernatural instincts of the uncivilized are toxic to the civilized and the peace and security in a civilized society. The civilized are required by the constitution to make decisions guided by our natural instincts because the civil nature represents law and order. It is not the correct interpretation and application of the constitution to fulfill this requirement when the supernatural pretend to be of the civilized nature .According to the guidance of the constitution the wrong identification, interpretation and application of the constitution is establishing and maintain lawlessness, which is creating hell on earth. According to the guidance of the constitution, the supernatural or the uncivilized are the only ones that can break the law or establish lawlessness by the misuse of their supernatural powers and senses. The way the supernatural create lawlessness is to undermine the constitutional authority of the civilized or the natural. The supernatural because of their impaired judgments associated with their supernatural instincts find it difficult to accept that the civilized do not want to have anything to do with them, even with clear revelations of the constitution on the subject. They keep on misusing their supernatural powers and senses to plan the lives of the civilized, illegally, to revolve around them by making the civilized dependent on them rather than independent as required by the constitution. This blatant disregard for the law jeopardizes the peace and security of the planet.

Contrary to the guidance of the constitution, the supernatural or the uncivilized want to get involved directly or indirectly in private decisions the civilized make, unsolicited. To be able to do this, the supernatural will have to force the situation by misusing their supernatural powers and senses. The supernatural phenomenon is unhealthy, intrusive and gives a false impression. The interests of the civilized are sabotaged by the supernatural, an example is the use of the internet, the supernatural use this interest to try to indirectly communicate with the civilized and it is illegal, unhealthy and gives a false impression. The civilized have no way of avoiding these intrusions through our interests, because we the civilized need the use of these things for our basic needs. The sabotage of these interests by the supernatural is an attempt to undermine the civil rights of the civilized; it gives a false impression, propaganda, it implies that the civilized need help constantly that we are incapable of taking care of ourselves which is a lie. This false impression has been illegally engineered by the supernatural to cater to their uncivilized nature, which implies that the supernatural or the uncivilized are by nature in constant need of help, looking for ways to spend their time, which involves crippling the civilized in order to create a lawless culture because it gives them something to do, at the expense of the mental and physical wellbeing of the civilized and at the expense of peace and security in a civilized society.

The supernatural or the uncivilized were pretending to be civilized and insisting that the civilized need to work or should be looking for work and entitlement to benefits is dependent on making genuine efforts to look for work, contrary to the guidance of the constitution. According to the guidance of the constitution, the civilized have dominion over this planet and every natural resources including money belongs to the civilized by right. The sadism of the supernatural or the uncivilized is evident in this practice of deceiving the civilized, in order to torture the civilized unnecessarily. This practice is evident in their version of the unconstitutional interpretation and application of the constitution. After this level of abomination, they are trying to misuse their supernatural powers and senses to give a false impression that their sadism is some sort of joke or game the civilized are playing with them. According to the guidance of the constitution, they need to ask themselves what the benefits are for the civilized to interpret our persecution as jokes and games. The civilized are by nature commissioners of police, in law enforcement, it is a symbolic acknowledgement of the constitutional authority of the civilized. In practice it is not work. The salary and uniforms are symbolic acknowledgements of the constitutional rights of the civilized. To interfere with these sacred rights of the civilized, is worse than deliberately severing someone's arms or legs or ears or trying to stop their breathing. The constitutional rights of the civilized are components of our nature; they cannot malfunction or be incomplete. If the supernatural or the uncivilized deny the civilized our constitutional benefits including salaries and uniforms identifying the civilized as commissioners of police for one misguided purpose after another, it is a serious act of terrorism and will be interpreted as the misuse of supernatural powers and senses to violate the civil rights of the civilized, which is an abomination and subject to punishments stipulated by the guidance of the constitution.

The massive differences in the natures of the uncivilized and the civilized, ensures that the right of dominion or the civil or administrative powers of the civilized provides an adequate balance or separation of powers to provide and maintain international peace and security. These civil powers can only be exercised by the civilized (those without supernatural powers and senses).

To undermine these rights, is an act of terrorism or are acts against humanity, which breeds lawlessness.

According to the guidance of the constitution, the supernatural or the uncivilized are not allowed under any circumstances to undermine or compromise the constitutional authority of the civilized, by trying directly or indirectly to interfere with the independence of the civilized or to compromise the right to self-determination of the civilized, by misusing their supernatural powers and senses to alter the constitutional living conditions of the civilized, which will have the effect of compromising the education of the civilized.

According to the guidance of the constitution, the supernatural owe the civilized a duty of care with regard to the approved constitutional living conditions required for the civilized to benefit from our civil rights. These constitutional requirements should not be confused with a paternalistic or maternalistic relationship with the civilized. The point of ensuring that the constitutional conditions are implemented is to eliminate the possibility of the supernatural interfering directly or indirectly with the independence or the right to self-determination of the civilized. The supernatural like to create problems in order to give themselves things to do at the expense of the mental and physical wellbeing of the civilized, the vulnerable and the peace and security in a civilized society.

The point of the constitutional requirement is to make sure that the supernatural are in no doubt who will be blamed for any adverse alterations to the approved constitutional living conditions meant for the civilized.

Given my civil nature, my experiences of the supernatural or the uncivilized confirms that the supernatural are extremely wicked, which is an understatement. This level of wickedness is not in line with the constitution's guidance on permission to have children. The current state of affairs will suggest that children are deliberately brought into this world to be tortured by the supernatural.

To determine the suitability of the world for children is if the conditions are aligned to the constitutional living conditions meant for the civilized.

The history of the United Kingdom with regard to the deliberate misinterpretation of the constitution, which is the Christian principles, civil rights and the deliberate unlawful persecution of the civilized, will suggest that their attacks on the civilized in the guise of jokes and games are being done with seriously hostile intentions.

If you consider very seriously their idea of God, which is a representation of their constitution, and what is possible with their supernatural powers and senses, then you will question their judgments with their creation of politics. You wonder about their judgments with their creation of religion, with regard to being worshipped by the harmless, vulnerable.

These creations by the supernatural or the uncivilized are unconstitutional, and breeds lawlessness.

The unwanted or uninvited emotional entanglements with the civilized by the uncivilized are very dangerous for the civilized because of the hostile supernatural instincts of the uncivilized. The civilized will by nature reject these unconstitutional dangerous emotional entanglements from the uncivilized, because it always leads to the misuse of supernatural powers and senses to harm the civilized mentally or physically.

It is amazing that with their supernatural powers and senses, the supernatural or the uncivilized are cowards that have to hide behind a constitution (civil nature) they are not to collectively torture the vulnerable or the civilized and try to claim that the attacks are occurring naturally. They behave like the cowards they are because they cannot legally justify these attacks on the vulnerable or the civilized.

The supernatural come into my home supernaturally, not in the physical form or in a civilized manner, for one misguided purpose after another, when the law expressly forbids this type of direct or indirect communication with the civilized. Not only does the constitution interpret these types of communications as unconstitutional, they are very unhealthy for the civilized.

When I was younger and unaware that I was surrounded by people different from me, because of the differences in their uncivilized nature (those with supernatural powers and senses), and my civilized nature (no supernatural powers and senses), they were hiding the differences and at the same time making my life hell by misusing their supernatural powers and senses to harm me mentally and physically. Surrounded by this nightmare, still unaware of the differences, my natural instincts led me to enroll in an Anglican seminary school. My natural instinct also led me to study law at university. After completing my studies my instincts led me to join the metropolitan police force in England as an Administrative Assistant even with an honors degree in law. I was still not aware that I was surrounded by those different from me with supernatural powers and senses. They were misusing their supernatural powers and senses to torture me mentally while I worked as an Administrative Assistant, these practices are the real crimes according to the guidance of the constitution. They misused their supernatural powers and senses at the metropolitan police force to talk to me indirectly, making me aware that they were aware of my private affairs without me disclosing it to anyone. This according to the guidance of the constitution is a criminal activity or practice. I was in a seriously confused state because at the time I was not aware of the differences in their constitution and mine, their supernatural nature and my civilized nature. They also failed to make me aware that an Administrative Assistant, if you are of a civilized nature, given the differences in their nature and mine actually means commissioner of police. The misuse of their supernatural powers and senses was so traumatic for me that I had to leave. It has to be noted that although I worked with people of different races at the metropolitan police force, those responsible for the direct misuse of their supernatural powers and senses were the white race. To force me out under those circumstances by the misuse of supernatural powers and senses undermines the real constitution and breeds lawlessness. The problem with this constructive dismissal, by the misuse of supernatural powers and senses, is that by nature the civilized are commissioners of police according to the instructions of the real constitution of the United Kingdom, which is the Christian principles, civil rights. In principle they are aware of the importance of the civil nature with the establishment and maintenance of law and order but the white race are not prepared to involve an official recognition of the importance, if you are not of the white race.

They have been doing everything possible since the constructive dismissal to give legitimacy to their unlawful decision by trying to misuse their supernatural powers and senses to alter my civilized nature. The problem they have had so far is that they need to make the compromise of my civilized nature appear to be consensual.

The white race have developed the principle of retaliation with the specific objective to undermine the rights of the civilized. If the civilized as constitutional law enforcement officers reject the demonism of the white race, they misuse their supernatural powers and senses for one misguided purpose after another, to harm the civilized mentally or physical as a type of retaliation to undermine the constitutional authority of the civilized in order to maintain and create lawlessness.

The white race see it as a challenge to revolt against a sacred constitution because of their prejudices.

It is quite alarming for me as a civilized person, that the history of the white race and those different from them, is one that involves the white race doing everything possible to strip away the self-respect and dignity directly or indirectly of those different from them. There is a difference between trying to help those you feel are less fortunate than you and oppressing, dominating them with the effect of stripping away their self-respect.

It needs to be noted that the misuse of supernatural powers and senses to persecute the civilized by the uncivilized involves the supernatural of all races, genders and ages. These practices establish and maintain lawlessness.

According to the current practice by police forces, police officers should be able to identify the constitution's definition of criminal activities in order to adequately protect the public from crime. Police officers, junior officers are required to be able to identify their senior officers. Part of their duties are to be able to make sure that their senior officers get their proper uniforms with the right ranks identifying the ranks of the senior officer and also to make sure their senior officers get their salaries at the right rate identifying their rank. So if they are not capable of identifying, interpreting and applying the constitution correctly, they will not be able to know the correct identities of their senior officers. And as a consequence they are operating outside the law, which makes them criminals and undermines law and order, which breeds lawlessness, which fails to protect the public from crimes.

When the supernatural misuse their supernatural powers and senses to try to compromise the constitutional authority of the civilized, it is an attempt at a coup de tat.

The star symbol is significant with regard to the relationship between the civilized and the supernatural. The star sign is used to identify Jewish people as a symbol of their special relationship with God. The star sign is used to confirm that someone is good. The star sign is used to identify law enforcement agencies or officers. The star sign gets its importance from its link to the civilized. The star sign originates from the differences between the civilized and the supernatural. The star sign signifies the enhanced sense of sight of the supernatural, as watching the civilized, and the civilized being of good character incapable of doing wrong given the differences in the natures of the supernatural and the civilized. The civilized are by nature commissioners of police, which the use of the star sign as a symbol of law enforcement by law enforcement agencies and law enforcement officers confirms. It appears that they are aware of the importance of the civilized with regard to law enforcement, when they do not have to face someone of a real civilized nature. They need to maintain order but not in its complete form. They are only prepared to apply the law in a limited form, which gives the uncivilized some type of organized anarchy, which caters to their barbaric nature and creates hell on earth. The law is sacred and must be applied in its complete

form or not at all, to establish and maintain law and order.
Most countries agree in principle that when lawlessness threatens the national security of a country, martial law is immediately implemented. The supernatural instincts of the uncivilized have blinded them to the extent of lawlessness which has crippled international peace and security. Although the supernatural agree in principle about the principle of martial law, they do not have the legitimacy to implement it and have been unable to identify the constitution's definition of criminal behavior or activity. To impose martial law, which is the purpose of the sacred constitution, you must identify, interpret and apply the sacred constitution. It also appears that the uncivilized are afraid of the real constitution and think they can ignore the law and come up with their watered down version with the extra objective of persecuting the real constitution's law enforcement officers, the civilized.

3. AUTHOR'S NOTES

This is my fourth non-fiction book about the law. It is about what I believe to be the correct identification, interpretation of the constitution of this planet. It is a no nonsense approach to law enforcement.

4. AUTHOR'S BIOGRAPHY

My name is Lord Loveday Ememe. I was born in the United Kingdom and of African origin. I live in Luton, England. I am a graduate of an Anglican seminary school. I graduated from the University of East London with a law degree.

Bibliography

THE BIBLE